E S S E N T I A L F I N A N C E

MANAGING CREDIT

W9-DAY-879

ROBERT MCKINLEY
AND
MARC ROBINSON

DORLING KINDERSLEY
London • New York • Sydney • Delhi • Paris • Munich • Johannesburg

A DORLING KINDERSLEY BOOK

Writing and Editing Stephanie Rubenstein
Design and Layout Hedayat Sandjari
Photography Anthony Nex
Project Editor Crystal A. Coble
Project Art Editor Mandy Earey
DTP Designer Jill Bunyan
Photo Research Mark Dennis, Sam Ruston
Indexing Rachel Rice
Editorial Director LaVonne Carlson
Design Director Tina Vaughan
Publisher Sean Moore

First American Edition, 2000
24681097531

Published in the United States by
Dorling Kindersley Publishing, Inc
95 Madison Avenue,
New York, New York 10016

Packaged by Top Down Productions

Copyright © 2000
Dorling Kindersley Publishing, Inc.
Text copyright © 2000 Marc Robinson

See our complete catalog at
www.dk.com

Dorling Kindersley Publishing, Inc. offers special discounts
for bulk purchases for sales promotions or premiums.
Specific, large quantity needs can be met with special
editions, including personalized covers, excerpts of existing
guides, and corporate imprints. For more information,
contact Special Markets Dept., Dorling Kindersley
Publishing, Inc., 95 Madison Ave., NY, NY 10016;
Fax: (800) 600-9098.

Library of Congress Cataloging-in-Publication Data

Robinson, Marc, 1955-
  Managing credit / Marc Robinson and Robert McKinley.-1st
American ed.
      p.   cm.
  Includes index.
  ISBN 0-7894-6316-4
    1. Consumer credit. I. McKinley, Robert. II. Title.
HG3755 .R58 2000
332.7'43–dc21   00-031827

Reproduced by Colourscan, Singapore
Printed by Wing King Tong, Hong Kong

CONTENTS

INTRODUCTION

F̲ew aspects of personal finance play as important a role in our financial health as credit. Virtually every one of us uses it. Many people use it every day. Good credit can make our lives more convenient and organized. Poor credit can have the opposite effect. Managing Credit is meant to give you the understanding to use credit wisely and to your best advantage. This book also presents guidelines for managing debt and dealing with the issues that arise when you're unable to repay what you borrow. Most of all, this book can help you build and maintain a good credit record, so you can have more of the things in life you might want, but not otherwise be able to afford.

THE CONCEPT OF CREDIT

If you understand what credit is and how it works, you will
be well on your way to using it to your advantage.

WHAT IS CREDIT?

Credit is an intangible thing you can't touch, see, smell, taste, or hear. Nevertheless, credit is something very valuable, yet fragile, because it is based on trust. It is a belief that others have that you can be trusted (or not) to keep your promise. If you have good credit, you are considered trustworthy. If you have bad credit, others may not trust you.

FOR LEVERAGE

You can buy things that you couldn't pay cash for by borrowing the money you need. For example, few people can pay cash for a home, but with credit, they can afford to buy something that might otherwise seem unaffordable.

FOR CONVENIENCE

You don't have to carry large sums of cash in your wallet to buy what you want, as long as someone is willing to trust your credit.

FOR BUDGETING

You can plan a budget and pay for things based on your future income. Knowing what you will be repaying each month makes money decisions and planning for the future easier.

DIFFERENT LOOKS ▶
*Like a chameleon, credit can
take on different appearances.*

CREDIT COMES IN MANY FORMS

Credit can be an opportunity as simple as a loan to pay for groceries (when you use your credit card at a grocery store), or as complex as buying a house (obtaining a mortgage). It can be:

- A loan where the money is paid to you, and you repay the bank;
- A loan where the money is paid to someone else, you repay the bank, and the bank repays that someone;
- A credit card, where you make purchases, the card issuer pays the merchant, and you repay the card issuer once a month;
- Other ways of paying for goods and services that don't actually require you to pay in full for the item when you receive it.

2 If you're credible you're believable. A credible witness in court is one who is trustworthy.

WHO CAN GET A LOAN BASED ON CREDIT?

Anyone who can prove to a lender that the money loaned will be repaid on time and in full. In other words, anyone who can be trusted to keep their promise.

1 Credit is a bridge between you and the things you want to buy.

HOW THE CREDIT SYSTEM WORKS

The credit world is a continuous cycle of borrowing and lending. To be able to keep the cycle going, everyone has to faithfully repay what s/he borrows. Every borrower who repays on time allows the lender to faithfully repay what s/he has borrowed, which allows the lender's lender to do the same—and so it goes. When someone breaks the cycle, the entire system suffers.

BUYERS

People like you often want a product or service that costs more than they're willing or able to pay using their own cash. So, they may find a lender (e.g., a credit card issuer or a bank), or ask the seller to arrange a loan for them.

SELLERS

People, such as store owners, need to make sales to stay in business, so they're willing to let you buy on credit. This allows sellers to make new sales and lenders to make new loans. In short, everyone can build their businesses.

DISCOUNT RATE

The Federal Reserve Bank charges banks this interest rate, which is always lower than the Prime Rate, so banks are assured of borrowing at a lower rate and lending at a higher rate.

LENDERS

Lenders make loans based on trust that their borrowers will repay faithfully. The interest they charge is their earnings. Once money is loaned, they may need to raise more cash to be able to make more loans. So lenders also borrow money from other lenders. Banks can borrow directly from the federal government. As long as a lender's cost of borrowing is lower than the fee it charges for lending, it can make money.

PRIME RATE

Lenders, particularly banks, charge their best customers (typically wealthy individuals and major companies) a low interest rate called the *prime rate*. They charge other customers higher rates, depending on the type of loan and each customer's own credit profile.

MONEY ISN'T ALWAYS CASH

Because of the credit system our society has a lot more buying power than it has cash. Of the entire U.S. money supply, which includes checking accounts, traveler's checks, and other checking-type accounts, less than 10% exists as actual currency. The remaining 90% is in digital form on computers. Reportedly, if you took the total number of actual bills in existence and spread them equally among Americans, each of us would have about $1,400.

BUSINESSES AND INDIVIDUALS

People like you make loans to the government every time they buy bonds, such as Treasury bonds. When you buy a bond, you're lending the bond issuer money and expecting to be repaid on schedule with interest. In short, if you buy a government bond and also take a loan from the government, you could be earning interest on the money you loaned to the government and using it to repay the loan you took from the government.

THE FEDERAL RESERVE BANK

The *Fed* is the federal government's bank. It lends money to banks specifically for the purpose of supplying them with enough cash to stay in the lending business. The Fed makes loans based on trust that the banks will repay faithfully (which depends partly on the bank's borrowers repaying them faithfully). When the Fed needs money, however, it can print more, raise it from taxes, or borrow it from the general public by selling bonds.

DIFFERENT RULES

The federal government can borrow as much money as it wants and doesn't have to go through a credit check to do it.

HOW THE CREDIT SYSTEM EVOLVED

The credit system evolved as lenders gave money to others in exchange for the promise of being repaid. Trial and error resulted in safeguards that reduce the lender's risk and encourage borrowers to repay their loans. This in turn created a larger pool of lenders to offer loans to borrowers like you. Here is a simplified version of how the system developed.

1. THE LOAN

You want to buy something but don't have the money. You ask to borrow someone else's money, promise to pay them back soon and tell them "you can trust me." The person says yes and becomes a lender. You borrow the money and pay it back whenever you feel like it. The lender realizes s/he received nothing of value in return for being without the money.

2. THE LOAN + INTEREST

The next time you ask for a loan, the lender thinks, "What's in it for me?" S/he agrees to make the loan only if you pay back the money plus a little extra (*interest*). You say, "I promise to pay you back with a little extra. You can trust me." You repay the money plus the interest, but you take a long time. The lender likes earning the little extra but isn't happy about losing control of the money for an unpredictable amount of time.

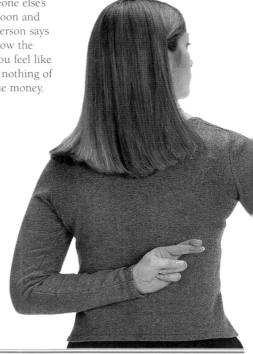

3. THE LOAN + INTEREST + DUE DATE

The next time you borrow money, the lender puts a time limit on the loan (a *due date*). You say, "Since it's harder for you to trust me, I promise to repay you plus a little extra, by a specific date." Once again, you repay late. In the meantime, the lender had a chance to buy something important, but lost the opportunity because s/he gave you the money.

▼ **PROMISES, PROMISES**
Loaning money is a risk. To protect themselves, lenders add restrictions to guard against broken promises.

4. THE LOAN + HIGHER INTEREST + DUE DATE

The next time you ask for a loan, the lender hesitates. You've broken your promise and damaged the trust. S/he says that since it's even harder to trust you, the only way s/he will let you borrow again is if you pay more than "a little extra" (higher interest) by the due date. You agree. But what if you're late repaying again, or you never repay? The lender charged higher interest, but didn't have either the interest or the money when s/he needed it. You've broken your promise again, and the lender has suffered again.

5. THE LOAN + HIGHER INTEREST + DUE DATE + SECURITY

You ask to borrow money one more time. The lender has two choices: (1) to say no, you're not worth the risk and you can't be trusted, or (2) to say yes, but since you can't be trusted, charge you a high interest rate and make you agree that if you don't repay on time, s/he can take some valuable property of yours and sell it to pay off the debt. So again you agree: If you don't keep your promise, the lender can sell your property to collect the debt.

Now, if you don't repay the loan as promised, you could lose your property (an appliance, car, home, or even the money in your bank account). In short, breaking your promise will cost you more money and can put your property at risk. Now that you feel the risk, you may be more careful to fulfill your promise—and the lender may feel more secure.

HOW YOU GET CREDIT

Credit is a reflection of you. It's a blend of your financial and personal qualities reviewed by lenders. A lender's offer of credit is an expression of trust in you that you will repay faithfully.

YOU APPLY

You ask for credit by completing an application. Here is the information you need to give the prospective lender.

CHARACTER

Part of trusting that you will repay what you borrow depends on your stability as a person and an income earner. For example, moving homes or changing jobs frequently, may indicate an unsettled, unreliable personality. It may also be a warning that the person could be hard to find should repayment become a problem. That's why many applications ask you to list all of your addresses and employers over the last three or five years.

 4 It's a federal crime to lie on a credit application.

WHAT IT ALL MEANS

Your credit profile doesn't make you a good or bad person, but it does make you a good or bad credit risk. Remember, though, lenders want to extend you credit because that's how they make money. They will only say "no" if they consider you too risky.

 3 The application is the official way you ask for credit.

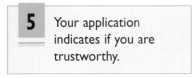

ASSETS

The things you own also yield insights. If you own a home, that speaks to your stability. Stock and other investments show you can save money, and they may possibly be an emergency resource.

> **5** Your application indicates if you are trustworthy.

RECURRING DEBT

Are there any other loans you've taken? How much do you already owe? How much credit has already been extended to you through credit cards and other lines of credit, even if you haven't used it yet? In other words, are you now, or could you possibly ever become, *overextended* (owe more than you can afford to repay)?

▲ PERSONAL PROFILE
Applications are the way you project your personal financial image.

INCOME

Your job history provides insights into your earning potential. It tells how much you've earned, whether there's been a steady increase, and the amount you're now earning.

MONTHLY EXPENSES

Your living expenses are your current fixed *overhead*. This amount is the minimum you can be expected to spend each month, excluding *discretionary* spending (money you spend any way you wish). This gives lenders a sense of the total amount your income will automatically be reduced each month. They then estimate how much will be left to repay your loan.

HOW CREDIT WORKS

O*nce you get credit, here is what you do with it. It's a continuous cycle.*

ACCEPT IT

From utilities. When you ask for electricity or a phone in your home, you enter the credit system. Since a utility can't know in advance how much electricity or phone time you will use, they let you use their product first and pay later.

From businesses. Businesses encourage you to buy on credit. You establish a relationship with them that makes it easier to sell things to you. When they send your statements, they can include new offers to you directly.

From home lenders. Homeowners are familiar with credit. They've received a mortgage. The government entices all of us to use this form of credit by offering America's single biggest tax break for individuals: tax deductions on mortgage interest payments.

USE IT

You buy from a merchant willing to trust your credit, and agree to pay the lender later. The lender pays the merchant. You can have what you want while you pay the lender for it.

OR

STORE IT

You can save your credit for when you really need it. This is called having *buying power*. By storing it, you can buy on the spur of the moment, beat a price increase, or take advantage of a sale.

6 Many employers check your credit before they make you a firm offer for a position.

7 Insurance companies review your credit before giving you auto or health insurance.

BUILD CREDIBILITY

How you repay debt shows whether you can handle credit wisely. If you repay faithfully and handle any problems conscientiously, you will most likely be offered more credit. As you use credit, your ability to borrow will either increase or decrease, depending on how you lived up to your promise. It's your responsibility to see that your ability to repay matches your ability to borrow.

Neglecting to make your payments and breaking your promise could make getting credit in the future difficult and keep you from buying the things you want and need.

REPAY IT

When you borrow money, you *go into debt*, and are required to repay what you borrow. You may or may not have to pay interest, depending upon the form of credit you use. Spreading payments over time will increase your cost of borrowing, because you will have to pay interest or other fees until you pay the money back. That's the cost of not having to pay cash when you buy something. It also allows you to budget and smooth out any anticipated rough periods.

THINGS TO KNOW

Here are ways you can use a credit card to build good credit:

- Use your card every month to make small purchases and pay off almost all, but not all of the balance, at the end of each month. If you can afford to pay finance charges, leaving a small balance to pay off will actually build a better credit rating;

- Use your card instead of writing checks. Credit cards, unlike checks, get recorded in your credit report;

- Pay your bill before the due date. This shows you are responsible, can be trusted, and it saves you finance charges.

8 Jobs where you will be handling money require you to have good credit.

YOUR CREDIT HISTORY IS REVIEWED

When you apply for credit, the lender checks on your credit history. This information first has to be gathered and put into a report. The report can be read by anyone who requests it to determine whether you have a good or bad credit record. Where does this information come from?

INFORMATION IS COLLECTED FROM...

Your application. This information becomes part of your file at the credit bureaus.

Businesses sending reports. Typically, any business that extends you credit or sells you insurance, sends the bureaus a monthly update on how well you are keeping up on your payments. It's an imperfect system. Not all businesses send reports regularly, and some only send reports to some of the major credit bureaus.

Public records. Any tax lien, court judgment, bankruptcy, or other legal event that could have an impact on your future ability to repay, or on your willingness to repay, goes into your file.

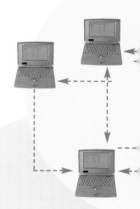

THE BIG THREE

The three national bureaus that control the national reporting system are:

- Equifax Credit Information Services;
- Trans Union Corporation;
- Experian.

Each bureau may have different information. You may, therefore, have three credit histories, not one.

---

9 A request for your credit report will appear on the report.

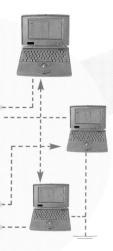

IT IS SENT TO...

National credit bureaus. Credit reporting bureaus collect information, collate it, and store it in their vast computer databases. There is no actual report stored on you. When there's an inquiry, the bureau draws all of your data from the computer and creates the report.

Local credit bureaus. There are several thousand local bureaus. Most receive their data from the national bureaus, although they may have more local credit information on you in their databases.

...REPORTS ARE SENT OUT

Under the Fair Credit Reporting Act, no one can see your report except you or someone with your permission. Reports show facts about your credit history. Some bureaus also provide business customers with *risk scores*. These scores are based on the facts in your report and indicate the likelihood of your going bankrupt or of chronically paying late.

Although all three national bureaus share information, they're still in competition for customers. Businesses pay to be members and have the right to order reports. Bureaus are careful about their members' legitimacy. Anyone who obtains a credit report under false pretenses may be fined thousands of dollars and jailed up to a year. In the end, your application for credit is either approved or rejected.

10 A rejection of your application won't be reported or appear on a later credit report.

What Goes into a Credit Report?

After they receive your application, lenders order a credit report on you to analyze your credit history. Typically, there are four categories of information in a credit report.

Personal Information

Included are items such as your name, current and previous addresses, marital status, Social Security number, date of birth, spouse's name, number of dependents, and employment information. This information may not seem worth reviewing, but you should check it carefully. All of this data combines to verify that the person in the report is actually you. It's not uncommon for files to be confused between two people with similar Social Security numbers or with the same name.

Lifelong Information

Though most information may stay on your report for no more than 10 years, a credit bureau may report your lifetime history if you are applying for:

● A job paying at least $75,000;
● Credit of more than $150,000;
● A life insurance policy with a face value of $150,000 or more.

Credit History

This is the record of how well you've kept your promises to lenders. It includes all current loans and many past loans. Account numbers, lender's name, amount borrowed, amount of last payment, amount still owed or the credit limit, and the timeliness of payments are all listed. A late payment (over 30 days) is a mark against you. If a collection agency has been used, it will read as a collection account (a mark against you even if listed as "paid").

MONITOR CAREFULLY

The time to check your credit report is before you apply for credit. It's better than waiting for surprises and discovering you've already been denied the loan.

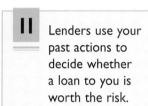

11 Lenders use your past actions to decide whether a loan to you is worth the risk.

PUBLIC RECORDS

If you've been in any disputes that have been serious enough to include the courts, prospective lenders want to know about it. These include tax liens, mechanics liens, court judgments, overdue child support, and bankruptcy. Any of these are negatives, even if they've been paid, because actions of this kind may indicate future troubles for the lender.

INQUIRIES

This is a list showing who else has requested a copy of your report. The list may go back two years (although a bureau only has to show inquiries from the past six months). It's common for a potential lender to turn you down because of excessive inquiries. Right or wrong, the thinking is that many inquiries may indicate you're asking many lenders to extend you credit. If so, it could lead to you falling deeply in debt and being unable to repay the lender reviewing your report. Review this to see if there are any requests you haven't authorized. You can ask to have unauthorized inquiries deleted from your report.

12 Your own inquiry to your credit report is not recorded on the report.

HOW LONG CAN INFORMATION STAY ON A REPORT?

The Fair Credit Reporting Act dictates how long a negative item can stay on a report.
- Lender inquiries: minimum six months;
- Employer inquiries: two years;
- Delinquencies, wage garnishments, repossessions, court orders, evictions for non-payment, and missed child support: seven years;
- Bankruptcy: seven or ten years (depending upon the type of bankruptcy you file) from the date of filing.

HOW TO READ A CREDIT REPORT

The information on these two pages gives you a head start toward understanding your credit report. Here's what you will find on most reports.

Account Number and Whose Account
This shows how you're responsible for the account.

Company Name
This shows who issued the loan.

NEGATIVE ITEMS ON YOUR REPORT

There are several ways you can deal with negative items on your credit report:
1. Pay off any balances and ask the creditor to update your records;
2. Wait for the information to be taken off your report;
3. Write an explanation of the debt and ask the credit bureau to add it to your report. This can be effective when dealing with debts that are the result of economic hardship or unemployment. The negative item will not be removed, but future creditors may take your explanation into consideration.

Personal Identification Informa

Mary Smith
555 Main St.
Town, State 99999

Credit Account Information

Company Name	Account Number and Whose Accou
1st Nationwide Mortgage	Individual Acc
Real estate mortgage Conventional mortgage	
American Express	Individual Acco
Credit card	
Citibank - VISA	Individual Acco
Countrywide	Joint Account
Real estate mortgage	
Express	Individual Accou
Charge	
First USA Bank	

Additional Information
This shows the type of loan. Any other information the lender feels is necessary is listed under the company name.

Date Opened
This shows when your loan account was opened.

Type of Account and Status
This shows the type of account and the payment status.

Last Activity
This shows the last time this account was used.

High Credit
This shows the highest amount you owed since the account was opened.

Call this number with questions -
Request Reference:
Report Date: 12 November 1999

CREDIT PROFILE

Social Security Number:
Date of Birth:

Terms
This shows the payment amount and/or the length of the loan.

Items as of Balance
This is the remaining amount due on the loan at the time the report was sent.

Date Opened	Last Activity	Type of Account and Status	High Credit	Terms	Items as of Balance	Date Reported Past Due	Date Reported
05/99	10/99	Installment Pays as agreed	$371K	$1935	$369K		10/99
06/86	07/99	Open Pays as agreed	$0		$0		10/99
10/84	09/99	Revolving Pays as agreed			$1994		09/99
193	04/99	Installment Pays as agreed	$410K	$2866	$0		05/99
95	05/95	Revolving Pays as agreed	$1000		$0		05/95
99	07/99	Revolving	$12000		$0		09/99

Past Due
This is any payment you have not made yet and is still owed.

Date Reported
This is the last time activity on your account was reported to the credit bureau.

POSITIVE AND NEGATIVE DON'T BALANCE

A large amount of positive credit doesn't usually outweigh items of negative credit. Any negative credit is an obstacle in the way of a lender's "yes" to your request.

THINGS TO KNOW

Joint credit is based on the assets, income, and credit history of both applicants. Married couples may get more credit this way, but will both be responsible for the debt—even if they divorce.

13

Reports from different bureaus may look different, but the kinds of information should be the same.

LOANS: THE CREDIT BENEFIT

If a lender is willing to trust you, you will get a loan.
The loan may come in the form of money, an authorization
card, or the ability to borrow at your convenience.

FOUR PARTS OF A LOAN

Although different kinds of loans have different terms, virtually every term falls into one of these four basic categories.

WHAT YOU CAN BORROW

The amount you borrow is called the principal. With some loans, you borrow it all at once. With others, you have a line of credit that lets you borrow up to a credit limit at any time.

With credit cards, for example, any principal you repay becomes immediately available to be borrowed again, as long as your credit remains in good standing. This agreement to let you borrow, repay, and borrow again is called revolving credit.

WHAT IT COSTS

Every loan has a cost. Although fees vary from loan to loan, the most common cost is interest (also called a *finance charge*). In most cases, payments are split. Part goes to repay the amount you borrowed, and part goes to pay the interest.

There may be other fees. Many card issuers charge annual fees, but they may waive it as a special promotion. Most cards have a fee for cash advances. Mortgage lenders usually charge up-front interest, called *points*, as well as fees for an appraisal, credit checks, and other work involved in setting up the loan.

14 Good credit gives you the ability to get a loan when you need it.

 15 In any loan document, the words "amount financed" simply mean the amount borrowed.

THE PAYMENT PLAN

A payment plan has three parts.
How much. Each loan is for a set amount or is up to a specified limit, at a specific rate. The interest rate or payment amounts may be fixed (stay the same each time), or they may be adjusted periodically. A loan agreement will state any adjustment schedule and the most the rate or amount can go up or down.
How often. Every loan must be paid back on a regularly scheduled basis. Most loans require you to make monthly payments.
How long. A loan may be for a day, a month, a year, or any time period set by the lender.

WHAT IF YOU DON'T REPAY?

Failing to repay on schedule can put you in *default*. Most lenders want to keep you as a customer. Polite reminders will become more serious requests if you don't pay. Some lenders may require that you put up some property you own as *collateral* (something they can take if you don't repay). This gives the lender some confidence that you will repay.

November 2000

Sun	Mon	Tue	Wed	Thu	Fri	Sat
			1	2	3	4
5	6	7	8	9	10	11
12	13	14	15	16	17	18
19	20	21	22	23	24	25
26	27	28	29	30		

SOMEONE TO HELP KEEP YOUR PROMISE

A *co-signer* is a person who signs a loan or credit card agreement with the primary applicant. The co-signer is responsible for repaying the balance of the loan or debt in the event that the applicant does not.

LOANS TO SUIT THE PURCHASE

Virtually anyone can lend you money, from an uncle or employer to financial companies. In practice, you could get a better deal if your choice of lender is based on your reason for wanting the money.

FOR A SPECIFIC PURPOSE

Some lenders will extend credit only if you will use the money to further their business. The purpose of the loan—the sale of the product—is more important than the loan itself.

Seller financing. Many department stores, retail chains, and car dealerships offer loans to help them sell products. They don't lend you the money, however. They arrange for you to borrow from a lender and may receive a commission for their effort. In effect, they sell you a product, and then sell you a loan to pay for that product. The lender legally owns the product (e.g., your car) until you fully repay the loan, and it can repossess the product if you fail to make payments on time.

Special interest financing. Mortgage lenders don't sell homes, but they will lend people money if it's used to buy a home. Since home loans are usually for large amounts, lenders require their borrowers to put up the home as security in case the loan isn't repaid.

▲ **BOAT LOANS**
People with boat or car loans don't own their vehicles until the loan is fully repaid. Until that time, the lender is the owner.

Lenders of student loans also insist you use their money for tuition and other education-related expenses. Since you're buying an education, however, there's no tangible property for you to pledge as security. Many student loans are government guaranteed to encourage lenders to make funds available to borrow and protect them if a loan isn't repaid.

FOR ANY PURPOSE

Some lenders extend credit without requiring you to specify how you will use the money. Their first consideration is whether you're pledging an asset as security; second, the quality of your credit rating; and third (if considered at all), your purpose for the loan. Here are some examples.

Asset-based loan. A bank, securities broker, or insurance company may let you borrow against the value of your insurance, home, or investments if your assets have enough value. Typically, these loans have lower interest rates than conventional loans. The lender reasons that if you own these assets, you've already exhibited financial responsibility and credibility. You're also protecting the lender by pledging assets of sufficient value to cover the loan in case you default.

Line of credit. This type of loan is a very useful tool in today's world although it's tempting to use it indiscriminately. You're given a credit limit (a maximum amount you can borrow). Then you're free to borrow up to that limit at any time for any purpose. Credit cards are the most common example, but home equity loans can also be lines of credit. Many banks offer lines of credit and use your checking or savings account as security.

Personal loan. You may get a loan on the strength of your name, or be asked to pledge an asset as security.

Pawning. Pawnbrokers lend money to anyone without checking credit. You bring in something of value, the broker lends you a small percentage of the item's value, and holds the item for an agreed period of time. You can pay off the loan within that time and reclaim your property. If you don't, the broker can sell it. Interest on these loans tends to be high. You may also be required to pay for the costs of insurance and storage.

16 The best loan for your specific needs may come from a lender who specializes in loans for the purpose you have in mind.

LEVERAGING WHAT YOU HAVE TO BUY MORE

To a lender, the most attractive borrower is one with proven financial responsibility or someone with assets under the lender's control. With these advantages, you can often get a loan more quickly and at better terms by leveraging the power of your assets.

YOUR HOME

One of the most tempting resources is your home's equity (the difference between what you owe and what the home is worth). Many lenders want you to have at least 30% equity (for example, you would owe no more than $70,000 on a $100,000 home, leaving $30,000—or 30%—as equity). In exchange for the loan, you give the lender a *second interest*. Your original mortgage lender has the first interest. If you fail to make the payments on the equity loan, the lender can force the sale of the home, even if your other mortgage payments are on time. There are two main ways to borrow against your home's equity.

Second mortgages give you a lump sum that you repay in scheduled installments.

Home equity lines of credit allow you to borrow any amount up to the limit, at any time, for any reason, and repay according to your agreement with the lender.

YOUR SECURITIES

Brokerage firms lend money *on margin*. This means that they will lend you money equal to a percentage of the value of the securites in your account. The firm gives you the loan, and you give the firm the right to sell your securities if you fail to repay. You pay interest on the loan and make payments in regular installments.

The attraction of margin loans is the interest rate, which is usually a few points less than you would pay at a bank. Margin loans can be risky, however. If the prices of your securities drop to a point where the securities' value doesn't cover the amount required to protect the brokerage firm, the firm will make a *margin call* (ask you to put in more money or pledge more securities). Failure to meet a margin call means an instant sale of the securities you've already pledged—even if at a loss.

YOUR LIFE INSURANCE

If you have a whole life policy (not term insurance), you may be able to borrow an amount equal to its *cash surrender value*. This is exactly what it says: the amount of cash you will receive if you decide to stop paying premiums and surrender the policy. The longer you own the policy and the more premiums you pay, the more the cash surrender value increases.

The interest charged on this kind of loan varies from company to company. Often, though, it's lower than a bank loan. An insurance company also isn't as concerned about being repaid. They will simply deduct what's owed to them before they pay your beneficiaries the remaining value of the policy.

BORROWING FROM A 401(K)

You can borrow from a 401(k). Different plans have different restrictions, and you will be required to make regular repayments with interest. So, not only will you borrow from yourself, you will also be paying interest to yourself. The downside of this is that you will have less money growing tax-deferred toward your retirement.

17 Better credit increases your chances of leveraging your assets for a loan.

SECURED LOANS

S ome loans require security. A lender has to believe that you will repay what you borrow. If the risk is too great to trust your promise, you will have to agree to a secured loan. The lender requires you to pledge an item of value they can sell if you don't repay the loan. Here's how it works.

THERE'S AN EXCHANGE

The lender gives you the loan and you give the lender the right to own a specific asset of yours if you fail to repay faithfully. If you're buying an expensive item on credit, such as a house, the item itself will be the secured asset. For other loans, a lender can ask for another item you own as security. It's up to you whether or not to agree to risk losing that item.

THE PROPERTY IS TIED TO THE LOAN

You give up the right to sell any property secured as part of a loan (called collateral) without the lender's written permission. If you deposit cash in an account as security, for example, you won't be permitted to withdraw that cash. Once you repay the loan, however, the lender no longer has any rights to your property.

IF YOU FAIL TO REPAY ON SCHEDULE...

You default on the loan, and by agreement, the lender can find other ways to collect the debt. Some lenders may be lenient if you make late payments. Others hold strictly to the terms of your agreement.

THE PROPERTY IS REPOSSESSED...

If the property is an appliance or a car, the lender may hire someone to come and take it from you. If it's your home, the law requires a *foreclosure* proceeding.

TWO MAIN REASONS FOR SECURED LOANS

1. The loan is for a large amount (the cost of a large appliance, a car, or a home).
2. Your credit record shows you haven't been repaying loans on schedule.

18

Lenders need a secured interest when they have a lot of money at stake.

THINGS TO KNOW

- Lenders who offer you a secured loan may not review your credit report as carefully. Since they know they can take something of value from you if you don't pay, they may focus more on how much cash, income, and debt you have.

- By law, creditors can't ask you to pledge as security any clothes, furniture, or other personal belongings unless they're the actual items you're buying on credit. Also, if your car is repossessed, you're entitled to anything left inside it (though you may only have this right if you call within 24 hours).

- If you still owe money after the lender takes your property, the debt will not go away. It becomes an unsecured debt. If you don't repay it voluntarily, the lender can try to have a court order you to do so. It's also possible that your wages will be *garnished*, meaning some of each paycheck will be paid to the lender instead of to you.

- Once a default is on your credit report, many lenders will refuse you new loans. Those who offer you credit will likely charge much higher interest rates to make their risk worthwhile. You may have to begin rebuilding your credit history by making small, secured loans, typically by getting a secured credit card with a low credit limit.

...AND IS SOLD

Your property may be sold at auction or as second-hand. If your home is *foreclosed*, you will be forced to move out so the lender can either auction it or sell it to someone else. The lender will use the proceeds to pay off as much of your loan as possible. Next, any other lender with a security interest in the same property will take what it's owed.

CREDIT CARDS

Credit cards are the most widely used form of credit. There is a credit card for almost everyone, each with its own unique offerings, benefits, payment plans, fees, and other features.

THE RIGHT PAYMENT PLAN FOR YOU

To choose the right card, consider how you wish to repay the money you borrow. With a good credit record, the choice is yours.

REPAY IN FULL: CHARGE CARD

Charge cards show that you've been extended credit, but only for short periods of time. This is usually 30 days. You're required to pay in full by the due date for any item that appears on your statement. There are, however, no interest charges. You will be charged a late fee if you do not pay in full by the due date.

FEWER CHECKS

In 1997, electronic payments had become so popular in Europe that the average German wrote 10 checks a year, compared to 83 for the French and 234 for Americans.

CARDS, CARDS, CARDS

The average consumer has 14 cards and a total outstanding monthly balance of over $7,000. About 43% of these pay off their entire balance each month, while 60% of co-branded cardholders pay off the entire balance each month. Co-branded card owners are often more interested in the rewards they will receive than they are in stretching out their payments.

REPAY AT YOUR OWN PACE: CREDIT CARD

This is the most popular form of card. It is an open line of credit you can use and repay at your own pace, as long as you make at least minimum payments. You can borrow up to a limit, and the amount you repay is immediately available to borrow again. This is called *revolving credit*. You may pay interest on what you borrow, or you may be given a period of time to repay in full without interest. It can either be:

Unsecured. Most credit cards are unsecured, which means a lender can't immediately take your property if you don't pay your bill; or,

Secured. People with poor credit or no credit history can usually receive a secured credit card through a bank (some retailers also offer secured cards). It looks and works like any credit card, with one main difference. You have to keep money in a savings account as security and allow the card issuer to tap into it if you fail to pay your bills. The amount of credit you receive is usually linked to the amount you deposit.

19 A credit card will work like a charge card if you repay in full each month.

PAY AS YOU GO: DEBIT CARD

If you don't want interest charges, can't get credit, or simply don't like buying on credit, you still can have a convenient way to pay. You can use a debit card, which doesn't actually give you credit. Instead, when you use it, your bank takes (*debits*) the money from your account and sends it directly to the merchant. If the money isn't in your account, the transaction will be rejected. ATM cards, used for banking at automated teller machines, are the most popular debit cards. Debit cards offer less fraud protection than credit cards. It's hard for the card issuer to recover money already paid from your account—and they pass on some of that risk to you.

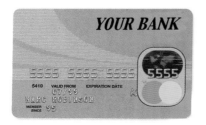

THE ANATOMY OF A CREDIT CARD

A credit card is an authorization card. It's proof that someone trusts you and has authorized you to buy on credit. Like a card that tells doctors you're insured, or a card that tells police you're licensed to drive a car, this card authorizes you to buy a product without cash. The card issuer promises to pay the merchant. The issuer then expects to be paid by you.

Valid from Date
This is the beginning date you can use the card.

Account Number
This number is embossed on the card, which makes an imprint possible and makes counterfeiting more difficult. The first digit identifies the company that issued the card. Each company has its own numbering formats. Many cards have the first four digits printed on the card below the embossed numbers as extra security. This prevents anyone from altering the embossed numbers. It may also have the full account number printed somewhere else on the card, such as on the signature authorization strip.

Your Full Name
This is the name you should give when placing credit card orders by telephone or other means. It's the name the card issuer uses to verify your identity when dealing with merchants.

Hologram
Almost all cards now have a holographic image that seems to move when you tip the card back and forth. The image is pressed on a color foil and contains ink that is only visible under an ultraviolet lamp. Holograms protect cards from being counterfeited.

20 Keep your card away from magnets. They could potentially erase the data on the magnetic stripe.

Expiration Date
This is the last date you can use the card. A card usually is valid for one to three years. If you maintain a good credit rating with the credit card company, you will automatically be sent a new card before your current one expires.

THE PIN

A PIN is a Personal Identification Number. To use your card for cash advances or withdrawals at an ATM, you will need to create a PIN: your password. Protect your PIN very carefully. Don't write it down, tell it to anyone, put it on the card, or let anyone overhear you repeating it.

WHO HAS CARDS?

On average, in 1998, people in these countries had these numbers of credit cards:
- Brazil: 2.1 cards
- Mexico: 1.9 cards
- Korea: 2.4 cards
- The U.S.: 5.6 cards
- Japan: 3.2 cards

Customer Service Number
For lost or stolen cards, or if you simply have questions about your account, call the number on the back of the card.

Authorized Signature Strip
You should sign the back of your card immediately when you receive it in the mail. This protects you from anyone using your card should it become lost or stolen. Your signature is one way to prove you did not make purchases that are in dispute. The signature strip on most cards is tamper-resistant. If anyone tries to erase your signature and forge their own onto your card, the strip will be destroyed, alerting merchants to forgery.

Magnetic Stripe
The black stripe on the back of every card is magnetic so it can interact with the electronic approval machine you see at most stores. The stripe contains your name, credit limit, PIN, expiration date, account number, and other data.

SPEEDY CREDIT

A credit card transaction between Japan and Hawaii takes less than a second to approve. The data travel at more than 4,464,456 kilometers/hour. That's 3,647 times the speed of sound.

21 Putting your picture on your card gives you added security.

THE COST OF A CREDIT CARD

Before you sign an agreement for a card, be sure you understand the basic costs you're accepting.

INTEREST RATES

Different cards come with different interest rates. The type of rate is set when you get approved for your credit card. The interest rate may be a fixed or a variable rate.

Fixed rate. Most cards offer a *fixed rate*, which means it does not change (unless the issuer changes the agreement). The rate you get charged each month is the *annual percentage rate (APR)* divided by 12. For example, if your fixed rate is 18%, you will be charged 1.5% interest a month.

Variable rate. Some cards offer a *variable rate*. This means the interest rate can change. Lenders must explain how they will adjust your interest rate, when the rate can change, how often it can change, and if there are any circumstances that could trigger a change. Many issuers who offer low introductory rates include a clause in the credit agreement stating that if you make a late payment, your rate can immediately adjust to the full rate. To check rates to be sure you're getting the right rate for you, see the *Money Rates* column of *The Wall Street Journal.*

22 The card issuer may raise your interest rate if you make a late payment.

23 Read the fine print on the inserts that come with your card. They may signal rate or fee changes.

OTHER FEES

Cash advances. Typically, interest charges begin the day of a cash advance. There is also a fee of between 1%-5% of the advance, or $5, whichever is more.

Annual fee. Some cards come with an annual fee that can be anywhere from $10 to $100 a year. If you don't want a card with an annual fee, you should ask the issuer about the terms on a card that has no fee.

Minimum finance charge. If you've passed the grace period, or haven't paid your balance in full, you will be charged interest. Each issuer will have a minimum charge, no matter how little money you actually owe.

Late payment. Paying beyond the payment due date may also cost you a late fee.

Over-the-limit. If your total balance goes over your credit limit, you may be charged a fee.

Returned check. If you pay your credit card bill by check and it bounces, you may be charged a fee.

Inactivity. Check to see whether your card issuer charges a fee for not using the card.

Account closing. Some issuers charge for closing your account or transferring balances.

THINGS TO KNOW

- Some card issuers charge a fee every time you check your balance or request other information through their toll-free customer service phone line. Be sure to ask about these types of fees when you apply for a card.

- On the back of each card statement is the cardholder agreement which tells you the fees on your card. Pay particular attention to any other items, which arrive with your statement, such as a Notice of Change in Terms. These may describe important changes to the fees on your card, such as how finance charges are calculated.

TEASER RATES

A common practice card issuers use to get your business is offering low introductory rates. These *teaser rates*, as they are sometimes called, usually look very enticing. Beware.

Short terms. The low rate is only offered for a short period, usually a few months. The quoted rate may be a monthly—not an annual—rate. Read the fine print to find out.

Compare adjustments. Your rate will adjust upward after the introductory period. Check to see if it will end up being higher than a rate you might get on a card without a low introductory rate.

Read carefully. The terms and conditions that come with the offer will list what ongoing rate you will get. This is the best way of protecting yourself from high interest rates.

UNDERSTANDING CREDIT CARD STATEMENTS

*Y*our statement is the best way to track spending, monitor charges, and catch errors. It's a snapshot of your account. Formats vary, but generally each statement includes the information shown on the next four pages. Your statement tells you:

24 The date the statement was printed is called the *closing date.*

Payment Due Date
The issuer must receive at least the minimum payment by this date or you will be charged a late fee.

Cash Advance Limit
You can only borrow this amount in cash. The rest of your credit can be used for purchases. Not all card issuers put a limit on cash advances.

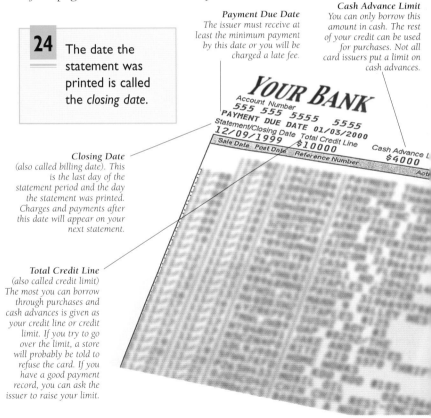

Closing Date
(also called billing date). This is the last day of the statement period and the day the statement was printed. Charges and payments after this date will appear on your next statement.

Total Credit Line
(also called credit limit)
The most you can borrow through purchases and cash advances is given as your credit line or credit limit. If you try to go over the limit, a store will probably be told to refuse the card. If you have a good payment record, you can ask the issuer to raise your limit.

WHAT YOU OWED AT THE START
Your statement tells you what you owed on the day the billing cycle began.

WHAT CREDIT YOU USED
All of your payments, purchases, cash advances, and other transactions are listed in the order they occurred.

WHAT YOU OWE NOW
The sum of what you owed at the start, minus the credit you used, determines what you owe now.

▼ **THE STATUS OF YOUR ACCOUNT**
The items listed at the top of this statement summarize the most important information about your account status.

New Balance
The amount you owed on the day the statement was printed.

Available Credit Line
What you could have borrowed on the day the statement was printed. This is the credit line minus the new balance.

Available Cash Limit
Your cash advance limit minus any advances you've made but haven't yet repaid.

With NO ANNUAL FEE

For Customer Service, call or write
555-555-5555 (5555)

New Balance
$5842.75

Available Credit Line
$4157

To report billing errors, write to this address; calling will not preserve your rights

Available Cash Limit
$4000

st Statement

Amount

Your Credit Use
This is a detailed list of each transaction, including payments you've made to the card issuer. It lists the date you made the purchase, the day it was recorded, the vendor, the amount of credit used, and various other identifiers.

WHAT YOU NEED TO PAY

Although different card issuers produce differently styled statements, virtually all provide you with the same pieces of information. Most also show how they calculated the charges at the bottom of their statement. Here's some help in understanding this important data.

25 Understanding how finance charges are calculated can save you money.

Purchases & Advances
What you spent and borrowed during the period.

Payments
The amount you repaid and, therefore, had reinstated to your credit line.

Finance Charge
The amount of interest charged this period.

Previous Balance
What you owed on the day your last statement (not this one) was printed.

Rate Summary
Here is where the issuer explains what your credit has cost you this past period, and how the cost was calculated. This information doesn't exist for charge cards since they don't charge interest.

Average Daily Balance
Buried in small type on the bottom of this statement is one of the most vital pieces of information; the amount used to calculate your interest. Each day, the issuer calculates your new balance by adding new purchases and fees and subtracting any payments or credits (see page 40 for an example of how this works).

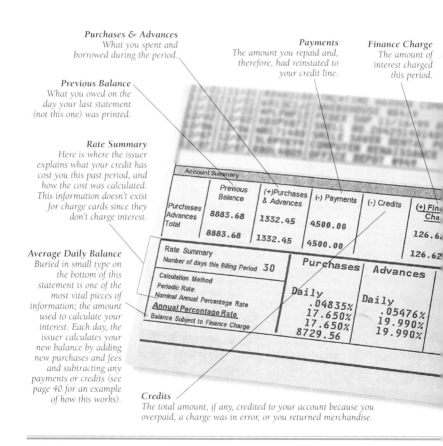

Account Summary					
	Previous Balance	(+)Purchases & Advances	(-) Payments	(-) Credits	(+) Fin... Cha...
Purchases Advances Total	8883.68	1332.45	4500.00		126.6...
	8883.68	1332.45	4500.00		126.62

Rate Summary		
Number of days this Billing Period 30	**Purchases**	**Advances**
Calculation Method	Daily	Daily
Periodic Rate	.04835%	.05476%
Nominal Annual Percentage Rate	17.650%	19.990%
Annual Percentage Rate	17.650%	19.990%
Balance Subject to Finance Charge	8729.56	

Credits
The total amount, if any, credited to your account because you overpaid, a charge was in error, or you returned merchandise.

26 Contact the card issuer immediately if you suspect any charges are not correct.

CALCULATING FINANCE CHARGES

No matter which type of interest you are paying, the finance charges may be calculated in one of the following four ways:

Average daily balance. This is the most common way to calculate finance charges. It takes your balances each day during the billing period, adds them all together, and divides by the number of days in the billing period. The periodic interest rate is then used to calculate the finance charge for that period (see the example, page 40).

Adjusted balance. With this method the card issuer subtracts payments you make during the billing period from your balance at the beginning of that period. This means your balance is kept lower and you pay less in finance charges.

Previous balance. This method applies the monthly finance charge to your beginning balance for the billing period. Purchases and payments during the month aren't included.

Ending balance. The card issuer may use your ending balance for the period. If so, any purchases and payments during the billing period are included.

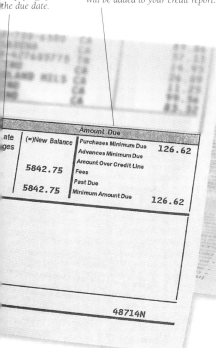

Minimum Amount Due
The least you're required to pay before the due date (which appears at the top of page under your account number). If you pay less than this amount, a negative mark will be added to your credit report.

Late Charges
This is the penalty for paying after the due date.

ate ges	(=)New Balance	Amount Due	
		Purchases Minimum Due	126.62
		Advances Minimum Due	
	5842.75	Amount Over Credit Line	
		Fees	
	5842.75	Past Due	
		Minimum Amount Due	126.62

48714N

39

CALCULATING CHARGES

T his is an example of how the finance charge (interest) is calculated on card purchases. Compare what happens when you make a large purchase at the start of a period. It can cost much more than when made at the end of a period. Notice how the average daily balance rises, even without new purchases, because there are more days with the higher balance outweighing the fewer days with the lower balance.

GRACE PERIOD ▼
Some issuers give you 20 to 25 days at the end of the billing cycle to pay the balance on your card. If you start the period with a $0 balance, (as in both scenarios here) and pay in full by the due date, you will pay no interest.

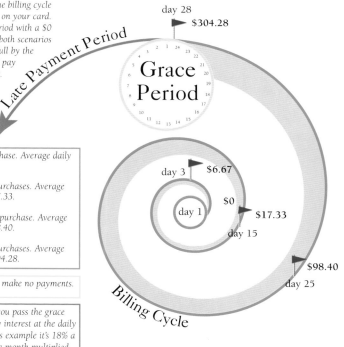

$4.56

Day 3. *A $20 purchase. Average daily balance = $6.67.*

Day 15. *No new purchases. Average daily balance = $17.33.*

Day 25. *A $2,000 purchase. Average daily balance = $98.40.*

Day 28. *No new purchases. Average daily balance = $304.28.*

Grace period. *You make no payments.*

Late payment. *If you pass the grace period, you will pay interest at the daily periodic rate (in this example it's 18% a year). That's 1.5% a month multiplied by the balance of $304.28 = **$4.56**.*

▼ HOW TO CALCULATE CHARGES

The calculation for finance charges is on the back of the statement. Most major card issuers use a method called average daily balance. *The issuer:*
1) takes what you owed each day;
2) totals all those amounts for the period;
3) then divides by the number of days in the period.

The finance charge is based on this. Most major issuers also use a daily periodic rate *to charge interest. Interest is added to your account daily, increasing your average daily balance even if you don't make any new purchases. Essentially, you're charged interest on the interest you owe and haven't yet paid.*

BILLING PERIOD

A billing period (or billing cycle) is the period of time covered on one statement, usually between 28 and 31 days. It may not begin at the start of a month or end at the end of a month, so you may buy something at the end of the month and it won't appear until the following month's statement.

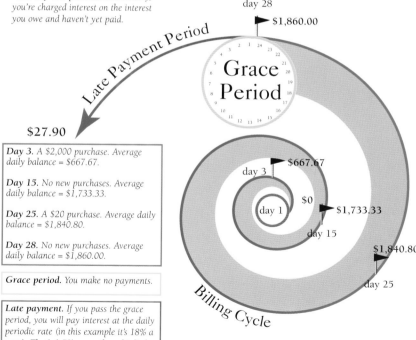

$27.90

Day 3. *A $2,000 purchase. Average daily balance = $667.67.*

Day 15. *No new purchases. Average daily balance = $1,733.33.*

Day 25. *A $20 purchase. Average daily balance = $1,840.80.*

Day 28. *No new purchases. Average daily balance = $1,860.00.*

Grace period. *You make no payments.*

Late payment. *If you pass the grace period, you will pay interest at the daily periodic rate (in this example it's 18% a year). That's 1.5% a month multiplied by the balance of $1,860.00 = $27.90.*

OTHER CARD BENEFITS

C redit cards come with other benefits besides credit lines. Depending on the card issuer and the level of credit you receive (for example, a standard, gold, or platinum card), you might receive added benefits.

EXAMPLES OF BENEFITS

The sales brochure and the introductory package will tell you which of these benefits are included with your card:

- Guaranteed hotel reservations;
- Double the manufacturer's warranty and extended service agreement on most products;
- Free collision coverage on auto rentals (no need to buy the agency's coverage);
- Travel and emergency assistance, including medical and legal referrals when traveling, arranging emergency transportation to hospitals, or travel for your children;
- Assistance with replacing lost tickets or luggage;
- Interpreters to help you in person or on the phone;
- Delivery assistance for prescriptions, valuable documents, emergency cash, card replacement;
- Trip assistance, from lists of ATM locations to weather reports and health and legal requirements in your destination;
- Travel accident insurance: $100,000 up to $1,000,000.

27 A good credit history will open you up to more benefits and rewards.

GOLD AND PLATINUM CARDS

Many card issuers offer premier versions of their credit cards to people with high incomes and/or excellent credit records. Gold and platinum cards typically offer:

● Higher credit lines, so you can buy more before hitting your limit;

● Benefits that are not available to standard card holders;

● A lower interest rate, although there might be an annual fee or no grace period.

THINGS TO KNOW

● Many cards come with offers, which are essentially insurance in case you cannot pay your credit card payment due to hardship. This could include involuntary unemployment, disability, or hospitalization. Be sure to evaluate the fees carefully to determine if this protection is worth it.

● You may be used to tossing enclosures such as the Disclosure of Changes to the Terms and Conditions of Your Card, but it pays to review them. Sometimes business conditions force issuers to alter the card's benefits or its fees. If you know what your card offers, you will avoid surprises at inopportune moments, and take advantage of new opportunities.

CREDIT REPORT MONITORING

Some cards come with a service, which will check your credit report periodically for negative items. It could be very valuable for maintaining a good credit history. The sooner you are made aware of negative items, the quicker you can address them and protect your credit record.

28 Some cards may cost more if they offer benefits or rewards.

SPECIALTY CARDS

Some cards offer special advantages. There is a card to meet just about any special interest or use.

SMART CARDS

Cards with computer chips in them instead of the magnetic stripe on the back are used widely in Europe, but less so in America. These are called smart cards, because they can easily carry a wide assortment of personal information which you control to suit your needs. You can load only the programs you want to add convenience and flexibility to your life. For example, you can load:

- Electronic cash as an alternative to cash. It is secure and convenient. Swipe your card through machines that accept it, and the cash is deducted from your card (not from an account);

- Travel preferences, such as seating and meals. If you use the card to buy a ticket, your preferences are included automatically;

- Health records loaded prior to a doctor visit. This ensures that your most accurate, up-to-date information travels with you;

- Discount programs from retailers and merchants you use. The discounts will be automatically calculated when you pay with your card.

SMART INSURANCE

People in Belgium use smart cards to access health insurance benefits, which reportedly reduces the cost of processing claims by between 65% and 80%.

29 Many specialty cards charge special fees. Be sure those fees are worth the advantage they offer.

REWARDS CARDS

Many cards have the name of a partner such as a major brand retailer or service provider, displayed on them. These are *co-branded cards* which give you a way to use credit and earn points toward a reward, a rebate, or some other benefit. Every time you use a card sponsored by an airline, for example, you may earn points toward free flights. A card sponsored by a car company may earn you discounts on a car purchase.

 30 Call your card issuer to see if they can switch you to a specialty card that works for you.

CASH BACK CARDS

Some card issuers give you cash back on the purchases you make. Check carefully to see what they are really offering you. For example, in one major promotion, a card issuer offers a 1% rebate on a year's worth of finance charges, not a year's worth of purchases. So, even if you spend $15,000 on the card in a year, and pay, for example, $275 in interest that year, you'd receive a $2.75 rebate.

AFFINITY CARDS

Card issuers offer cards that carry the logo of all kinds of associations and organizations. These are called *affinity cards*. Consumers usually want to have these cards because of an emotional, intellectual, or psychological attachment to the group or lifestyle represented on the card. If you like AARP, for example, then you might want an AARP-branded card. An affinity card sponsored by an association might mean that every dollar you spend generates a small donation to a worthy cause—or, for example, to your favorite sports team. There are affinity cards to interest virtually anyone. Check the terms to see whether you will be paying higher fees or rates than your current card and whether the tradeoff is worth it to you.

SHOPPER POLL

In 1997, shoppers were asked if and how they would use a smart card. More than half said they would use a smart card and most knew exactly how the cards would be used.

SECURED CREDIT CARDS

A secured credit card has something of value pledged against it. It will typically have a higher interest rate than other cards because of the risk the lender is taking with you. The card looks just like any other credit card, so no one will know its secured. Here's how it works.

ACCEPT THE CARD

It's a *secured* card because it's tied to something of value that you own. This is usually a savings account. You usually pay an amount up front to the credit issuer for a limited amount of credit. If you don't pay (default on) your debt, the issuer has the right to take the cash you owe from your account. This reduces the lender's risk of lending the money to people with credit problems.

SEND MONEY

Typically, the card issuer sets up a savings account and you send the amount of money, by check or money order, that the card issuer requests. The amount is usually related to your credit limit - sometimes less. Many issuers, however, offer bonuses that increase your spending limit from 50% to 100% over the amount you deposit.

31

Use a secured card to establish or rebuild your credit record.

BACKING UP YOUR PROMISE

You may see your property identified as the lender's security or collateral. For secured cards, the money you deposit in a savings account is the collateral.

VARIATION ON A THEME

Some card issuers offer unsecured cards to consumers with poor credit. These cards cover the risk by charging hefty upfront fees and a high annual interest rate. For example, you may receive a credit limit of $250 in exchange for $200 in fees. Weigh these offers carefully.

REESTABLISH CREDIT

If you build a record of good payments, the card issuer may eventually give you a higher credit limit. After a while (for some issuers, its about 18 months), your secured account may even be switched to an unsecured account. You would then be free to use the account without needing money in an account to back up your repayment promises.

MAKE PAYMENTS

Your payment terms will be specified by the card issuer. Check all the terms before you accept the card to be sure you understand the agreement. Remember that you have been issued a secured card because the issuer does not trust that you will keep your promise to pay, without the security. Paying in full, before the due date will help rebuild the issuer's confidence in your promises.

WHO MAY NEED A SECURED CARD

Card issuers focus on your job, income and debt status, and past credit history to decide whether to trust your ability and willingness to repay. If a lender declines to offer you an unsecured card, you may be offered a secured card instead. There are two types of secured credit cards.

Fully secured card. A fully secured card is one where the credit limit equals the amount deposited in the specified savings account. This card is offered as a way to build credit.

Partially secured card. Some secured cards are only partially secured. The amount of security lenders ask for depends upon the level of risk they feel they are taking.

KNOW YOUR CARD RIGHTS

Y our card rights are listed on the back of every statement in the cardholder agreement. Important among them are your rights to correct problems.

32 The phone number for reporting a lost or stolen card is on the back of every statement.

33 The Fair Credit Billing Act protects you from errors and fraud by merchants when using your card.

UNAUTHORIZED USE OF THE CARD

Report theft immediately. If you report theft immediately, you're not liable for any transactions made without your consent. If you report the card missing within 30 days, you're only liable for up to $50. If you call within two days, generally the liability is zero.

Card protection. Many card issuers offer a lost or stolen card protection service for a fee (typically $25 to $40 a year). When considering whether this is worth the fee, keep in mind liability is limited to $50, as long as you call your card issuer.

Disputes on your card. During a dispute, the card issuer may not report the amount to a credit bureau as a delinquent payment, and no collection agency can come after you. The issuer can continue to tally interest charges against the amount (in case you end up owing it), and they can reduce your credit limit by that amount.

Not satisfied. If the situation isn't settled to your satisfaction, you can notify the issuer in writing within 10 days. Then, if they report it to a credit bureau as a non-payment, they're required to include your side of the story, as well.

Billing Errors

If you find an error on your statement, you can withhold payment on the amount (or ask for a credit if you've already paid) while the card issuer investigates the problem. You must notify the customer service department in writing, not by phone, within six months (60 days for debit cards) of the billing date (also called the *closing date*). Include any evidence, such as receipts and letters that support your claim.

Once notified, the company has up to 30 days to respond to you, and up to 90 days to resolve the problem. If there's no resolution within 90 days, you can deduct $50 from the amount even if you lose the dispute.

Debit cards don't provide as much protection as credit cards.

Defects or Disputes

By law, every product must work properly if used for its intended purpose. When you buy a product with a card, you get a form of insurance or *buyer protection*, which helps you dispute charges that are:

● Above the agreed-upon price;
● For items ordered but never sent;
● For wrong items;
● For items that don't work as they're supposed to;
● For unsatisfactory services.

Buyer protection applies to any purchase over $50 you made in your home state within 100 miles of your mailing address, or over the Internet. In other words, it doesn't apply to purchases made during far-away vacations. If the card issuer advertised the product or owns or operates the business selling the product, there are no minimums on money or location.

Try to resolve the issue directly with the seller. If that doesn't work, you can refuse to pay the bill and ask the card issuer to step in. The issuer must try to resolve the issue within 90 days. If it takes longer, you may not be liable for the charge at all.

PROTECTING YOUR CREDIT

There are many ways you can protect your credit.
The most important thing is to be aware of your credit
history and how to avoid problems that may arise.

MONITORING YOUR CREDIT REPORT

*H*ere are some ways you can correct
errors in your report.

1. SEE YOUR REPORT

You're entitled to see your credit report at any time. A report will usually cost $8.00. In Maine or South Dakota, they're $2.00 each. In some states, such as Maryland, they're free.

2. WRITE, DON'T PHONE

The safest way to make a request is in writing. Phone calls often lead to a recorded message system. If you reach a person, don't try to resolve the dispute over the phone. It may only confuse the issue or make it worse. Write down your issues and review them carefully, so you're sure you're stating your case clearly.

3. SEND IT CERTIFIED MAIL

Send the request letter certified mail, return receipt requested. The post office will tell you how to do this, if you don't already know. Copy the letter and the check for the report. Date and file them, so you can refer to them later if necessary.

4. WAIT 3-4 WEEKS

If you don't get a response, you should send another letter certified mail, return receipt requested. State that you've waited the proper amount of time and that you expect to see your report in your mail. Include copies of your first letter and your cancelled check.

5. IF YOU DON'T GET A RESPONSE

If there's no response from the bureau within thirty days, call them and ask to speak directly with a Customer Service Manager at the bureau. Get the name and title of each person with whom you speak. Discuss what you need and the time frame for completion. Follow up with a letter to the manager covering the agreement made during your phone conversation.

6. REQUEST A REVISED COPY

You're entitled to a copy of your corrected report at no charge. By law, the bureau must also send corrected copies to anyone who has inquired within the last six months. If you don't get a corrected report, write to the bureau stating that you want a free copy of your corrected report as entitled by law. Send a copy to the Federal Trade Commission. This should assure that you receive the revised copy of the report.

7. ADD YOUR OWN COMMENTS

You are entitled to include a 100-word statement of your own in your credit file. Use this right carefully. Some experts say that, in practice, potential lenders rarely read them. What's more, you may unknowingly verify a negative item on the report.

35 The Equal Credit Opportunity Act protects you by restricting what bureaus can report.

THE REPORT MAY BE FREE

A lender who refuses to give you credit must include the reasons for the denial in writing. You may write to the credit bureau listed on the denial letter, within sixty days of being denied credit, and request a free copy of your credit report.

36 You may dispute your credit report if you believe it's unverifiable, inaccurate, or obsolete.

37 Credit bureaus can't reveal race, religion or criminal records.

HELPFUL HINTS FOR PROTECTING CREDIT

*Y*ou could probably use some helpful hints. Credit experts offer these tips for removing inaccuracies from your credit report.

MONITOR CAREFULLY

The time to check your credit report and fix anything that needs fixing is before you apply for a loan. It's a lot better than waiting for surprises and discovering at the last minute that you've been denied the loan.

CORRECT PROBLEMS

It can be risky to correct problems on your credit report yourself. You could make matters worse if you're not well organized and precise in your dealings with the bureaus. Contact a credit counseling group for help if you don't feel comfortable doing it yourself. Some experts believe the risks include:

- Using forms from self-help books that may lead to misleading statements or lies, or that won't be taken as seriously as a personal, typed letter;
- Confirming, or even adding new, negative information unintentionally;
- Making statements that trigger an alert for fraud or other concerns;
- Wasting time on strategies that experts know won't work.

LABEL THE DISPUTE

Always clearly indicate in writing whether you're challenging an entry because it's "not mine" or "not late."

CHECK FOR ERRORS

Experts advise you to look for common errors such as:

- Items that belong to someone with the same name or similar Social Security number;
- Duplicate information;
- Not removing items that have been proven wrong or are past the time required for them to be carried on your report.

38 In most states, it's a crime to lie in a credit report dispute.

REMOVE UNAUTHORIZED INQUIRIES

By law, anyone with "legitimate business needs," can request a copy of your report. This includes employers, car dealers, home loan companies as well as other legitimate lenders, even if you didn't give a written release authorizing the inquiry. Be cautious about giving out your personal information, even if it is a casual conversation.

THINGS TO DO

- Make a list of all your credit cards and other important identification and keep it in a safe place, such as a safety deposit box. Include the card issuer's name, your account number and the customer service phone number of all your cards. In an emergency you may need to refer to this list quickly. Having to reconstruct this list after your cards have been lost or stolen could be very frustrating and time consuming and may cause you further delays in securing your credit from theft.

- When dealing with a dispute, keep a file of copies of all letters, mark your calendar for important dates, take down names and titles of every person with whom you speak. Keep a log of what is said. Send letters by registered mail to have proof of the date and location your letter was received.

- If someone is using your ID to get credit, you may want to write the credit bureau, list the fraudulent accounts, and ask the bureau to put a fraud statement in your file. This will alert future lenders to call you before granting any new loans. Contact the lenders of those illegal accounts and ask for an "Affidavit of Forgery." Complete it and send it to the credit bureaus. The bureau will only begin its investigation after receiving it. Give the process about 30 days from the time you send back the affidavit. Follow up if necessary.

◀ **INTERNET FRAUD**
With the advent of the Internet, unauthorized requests for credit reports have increased.

QUESTIONABLE CREDIT PRACTICES

B *uyer beware. Here are examples of practices that are unfair, misleading, or illegal.*

MINIMUMS AND DISCOUNTS

This isn't unfair, misleading, or illegal, but it's valuable to know. Most card issuers don't let stores require minimum purchases. In some states, stores can offer a discount if you pay in cash. But they can't charge more than the retail price if you use a card.

> **39** Consumer credit counseling services can verify the authenticity of a credit issuer.

PERSONAL INFORMATION

Many businesses may want your address or phone number for their mailing list, or to sell to a direct mail company. Most card issuers forbid merchants who accept their card from conducting this practice. You may be required to show a picture ID, but experts recommend not letting anyone write down your drivers license number, especially if it's also your Social Security number.

PRE-APPROVAL OR GUARANTEED APPROVAL

Some ads guarantee you will be approved for a card no matter what your credit history or how little you deposit in a special account. These should be reported to your state's consumer protection agency. Also, be suspicious of people who want a fee for getting you a card. You can do it yourself. Another caution: Some guarantees end up being approvals for a tiny credit limit (e.g., $100). The issuer then checks your credit profile, and if it shows problems, refuses to raise your limit. Be aware, there may also be an application fee, annual fee, late charge, and other expenses that could add up quickly.

PHONE CALLS

Don't give your credit card number out to anyone over the phone that has called you. Ask them for information such as their phone number or other identifying information so that you can check out their references for yourself. Any legitimate credit issuer will be able to give you information to easily check on their credibility.

LOOK-ALIKES

Some ads offer cards that look a lot like a major brand card but are merely similarly colored cards you can only use to shop through a specific catalogue, often at higher prices. Look at the offer for a brand mark you recognize to be sure of what's offered.

CONTESTS AND PROMOTIONS

There are many scams (and legal but misleading marketing campaigns) that guarantee you've won a prize with no obligation to buy, or offer tremendous discounts if you call right away. These people are usually either trying to get your credit card number so they can use it, or slowly lure you into using your card to buy their product (at an inflated price or one which you never receive). This is a big problem area for law enforcement and consumers because the offers seem so tempting that people want to believe they're winning something for free, despite their better judgment.

A REAL STINKER!
Push the load out of sight into a cigarette. When it starts to burn, tastes awful and smells worse. Sure to stop moochers.

Stinko Loads

40 In many states it's illegal for stores to write your credit card number on your check.

Disappearing

1 OUNCE

WHERE TO COMPLAIN

If you think a store has been unfair, you can report them to your state or city consumer protection office or attorney general. The card associations also want to know about violations of their rules. Start with a call to the bank that issued your card. If you aren't satisfied, try the card association, such as MasterCard or Visa.

Managing Your Debt

How much debt can you handle? The answer is different for everyone. How you handle debt can affect you for a long time. Pay attention to the advantages, pitfalls, and consequences of debt.

The "Right" Amount

Many experts recommend that no more than 15-20% of your monthly household take home pay be committed to credit card minimum payments and other loan payments, excluding rent or a mortgage. Furthermore, no more than 40% of your monthly take home pay should go to paying all debts, including rent or a mortgage.

What Is Right for the Lender

Most lenders have a level of comfort with your credit. They will lend you only as much as they feel they can risk. Typically, they will lend you:

- 37% of your current income;
- 28% for a home;
- 9% for other debt.

NO TURN ON RED

STAY OUT OF THE RED ▶
A sure way to manage debt is to try to stay out of debt entirely—something not too many people can do these days.

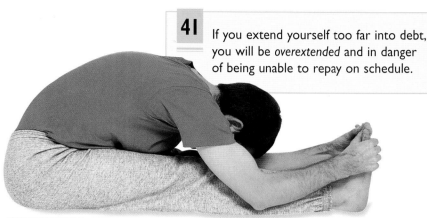

41 If you extend yourself too far into debt, you will be *overextended* and in danger of being unable to repay on schedule.

THINGS TO KNOW

Some experts figure out how much you should use your credit to take on debt, by calculating what is called a *credit ratio analysis*. This is also a measure of your financial abilities. The ratio is calculated by dividing your monthly expenses into your income.

● A low ratio is under 20%, which means that the person is in good financial health and is doing a good job of managing finances;

● A moderate ratio is between 21% and 40%. This may mean that the person should look carefully at their monthly payments and expenses and start decreasing their overall level of debt, including credit cards;

● A high ratio is over 40%. This may mean that the person should immediately stop accumulating debt and start looking for ways to decrease his/her total debt level.

WHAT IS RIGHT FOR YOU

In order to determine what amount of credit is right for you, follow this calculation:

Income. Add up all your income for one year, whether it comes from a job (after taxes), loans, scholarships, parental or spousal support or any other source. Divide this number by 12 to get your monthly income.

Expenses. Add up all your expenses including rent, loan payments, car payments, insurance payments, clothing, transportation, utilities, and any other expenses you usually have during one month.

Extra. Subtract what you spend (expenses) from what you make (income) to determine how much you have left over each month.

For example, if you make $2,000 per month and you spend $1,500, you will have $500 left over. You may choose to save this money, or you may choose to leverage your buying power, by taking on a loan, which costs you less than the $500 per month.

GETTING HELP WITH DEBT

I f you can't resolve a debt directly with a creditor, or you're not sure what to do, consider enlisting help from a credit counseling service. Here are some that can help.

WHO TO CONTACT

You can trust any service associated with non-profit organizations:

- Genus Credit Management is a non-profit, national service offering free debt counseling over the phone;
- Debt Counselors of America (DCA) is the first Internet-based non-profit credit counseling firm;
- Consumer Credit Counseling Service (CCCS) is supported partly by the credit industry. For a small fee (waived in hardship cases), a counselor acts as a go between with your creditors and helps set up a workable repayment plan;
- The National Foundation for Consumer Credit (NFCC) is dedicated to educating consumers in the wise use of credit. The NFCC is the parent group for the CCCS;
- Universities, military bases, credit unions, and housing authorities may also offer low or no cost credit counseling programs.

42 Get help quickly. Waiting will usually make your situation worse.

OTHER OPTIONS

If the consumer counseling services aren't helpful, you have other choices. They are:

Mediation. Becoming more popular is the use of a neutral third party to help you and the creditor open a line of communication and resolve your dispute. It's very informal. The mediator can't force either side in the dispute to do anything;

Arbitration. You and the creditor may agree to argue a disputed charge before a neutral third party (often a lawyer or judge). If the dispute isn't over much money, the process is informal and probably won't require a lawyer. Both you and the creditor are bound by the decision (and the winner may also win a refund of the arbitration fee);

Litigation. This is the most expensive and most aggressive choice. A lawyer can negotiate or fight a legal battle for you, if necessary. For example, you can tell a collection agency to speak only with your lawyer if you want to avoid calls at home.

HOW A PLAN WORKS

Through a Debt Management Plan, the counselor creates a workable budget with you and negotiates with creditors to reduce your monthly payments and extend the time to make payments you've already missed. They may also be able to negotiate waived or lowered interest rates while you're on the plan. Each month you send your counselor the amount necessary to pay your creditors. They hold it in a special account and mail checks to your creditors weekly. You will be required to close existing credit lines and receive no new credit until your debts are under control.

43 The best way to reduce debt is to earn extra income and reduce expenses.

COLLECTION PRACTICES

If all else fails, a lender will turn over your account to their collection department or a collection agency.

WHEN YOU DON'T PAY DEBTS

The last resort of any creditor, other than suing you (which may not be economically feasible), is to hand over your debt to a collection agency. These people are not interested in keeping you as a customer. The collector may start by sending you a notice. If you don't respond, phone calls will begin. You can try to work out a repayment plan with the collector, and if you get nowhere, you can try to contact your creditor again and explain your plan. Many of these agencies will use aggressive tactics. By law, there are limits, however, to what they can do or say to collect from you.

44 Lenders pay collection agencies to recoup as much debt as they can— not to help you.

USEFUL TIPS

Here are some suggestions for handling debt collectors.
Never get angry. Losing your temper with a debt collector may only make your situation worse.
Never send a postdated check. It makes your payment offer conditional and doesn't help resolve the problem.
Document all conversations. Include the name of the collector you spoke to, the date and time of the phone call, and exactly what was discussed and resolved.
Get everything in writing. Have the collector mail or fax the agreed upon settlement to you immediately.
Try negotiating. Try to settle the debts for 1/2 to 2/3 the amount you owe. The collector will still make money and you will save money.
Hang up if necessary. If a collector becomes abusive on the phone, do not stay on the line.
File a complaint. If your rights have been violated, file a complaint with the Federal Trade Comission. However, you will still need to resolve your debt.

THE CONSUMERS BILL OF RIGHTS

Bill collectors are restricted by the Fair Debt Collection Practices Act, which applies to everyone who collects consumer debt for someone else, including attorneys. Here are some of the laws:

- You have the right to tell a collector not to contact you again. After that they can only call to say collection efforts have ended or that you're going to be sued;
- If you don't come to an agreement with a collector, their only option is to hand your case back to the creditor or the creditor's attorney;
- Collectors can't threaten violence, or use obscene or profane language;
- Collectors can't contact you at work, and they can only call you at home between 8am and 9pm. Even then, they can't harass you on the phone;
- Collectors can't put any markings on the outside of a letter or other communication (such as a postcard), which would reveal they're trying to collect a debt;
- Collectors can't mislead you into repaying a debt.

CONSOLIDATION LOANS

*Y*ou may want to consolidate your debts into a single loan. If you are having difficulty paying your debts, there may be some advantages to getting a consolidation loan. It all depends upon your specific situation.

WHY USE ONE

A consolidation loan merges your existing loans into a single loan. This type of loan creates one payment for all your debts and can reduce the amount you owe.

One advantage is that if you can successfully consolidate your loans, you may be able to avoid bankruptcy. Under loan consolidation, a company negotiates with your creditors for you and gets the lowest possible monthly interest rate and minimum payments they can.

Why would a creditor want to do this? Remember, it's to their advantage to help you pay your loans back. They would rather have a reduced rate, especially where they are still profiting from your loan, than to receive nothing at all and have to sue you to get their money back.

Best of all, this all works to your advantage. Your payments are reduced. You only have to make one convenient monthly payment to the consolidation company for all the loans they're able to consolidate. The creditors pay for the consolidation, and you're rebuilding your credit in the process.

 45 Be careful who you select, some consolidators are not reputable.

WHO RECEIVES OFFERS

Lenders send loan consolidation offers to anyone whose name and address they can get. It doesn't mean the lender knows anything about you or your credit history yet. In most cases, you still have to fill out an application and be evaluated as you would for any other loan.

 46 Spending the money you've saved by consolidating debt will only increase your monthly payments again.

EVALUATE THE OFFER

Below is a typical example of a loan consolidation direct mail offer. To begin analyzing an offer, see whether it provides information on the four basic parts of a loan (see pages 22-23).

1. How much can you borrow? In this case the lender is willing to let you borrow $60,000 dollars.
2. What will it cost? The annual percentage rate (APR) here is 13.38%.
3. What is the repayment plan? Your payments will be due once a month.
4. What if you don't repay? This offer does not give this information.

There is a lot of other information missing from this offer. Read the fine print, and check out the lender and the offer carefully to be sure you completely understand what you are getting into.

THE HOME EQUITY LOAN

Many loan offers for debt consolidation are actually home equity loans. Lenders feel safer offering you a relatively low rate loan (or a higher rate loan if your credit record has trouble spots) because you're required to put up your home as security. They may try to entice you by claiming the interest on a home equity loan is tax deductible. Some or all of the interest may actually not be deductible. Consult your tax advisor first.

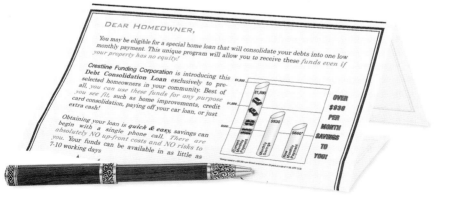

DEAR HOMEOWNER,

You may be eligible for a special home loan that will consolidate your debts into one low monthly payment. This unique program will allow you to receive these funds even if your property has no equity!

Crestline Funding Corporation is introducing this Debt Consolidation Loan exclusively to pre-selected homeowners in your community. Best of all, you can use these funds for any purpose you see fit, such as home improvements, credit card consolidation, paying off your car loan, or just extra cash!

Obtaining your loan is *quick & easy*, savings can begin with a single phone call. *There are absolutely NO up-front costs and NO risks to you.* Your funds can be available in as little as 7-10 working days

OVER
$930
PER
MONTH
SAVINGS
TO
YOU!

TOO MUCH DEBT

What if you feel like you're over your head in debt? Find a way to get out of it. Making an effort to pay your bills will help lenders see that your promise is still worth something.

CONTROL DEBT

Experts suggest a few ways of reducing or controlling debt from the start.

Refinance high-cost loans. Refinancing high interest rate loans can immediately reduce your payments.

Build an emergency fund. Having three to six month's expenses in the bank can prevent disaster. If something happens to you, such as unemployment, disability, or hospitalization and you have no income, this will help pay your expenses while you get back on your feet.

Make a budget. Start by writing down all the ways you spend money, including small cash expenses. If you can't pay your debts, see which expenses you can cut back or even eliminate altogether.

Pay off high-interest debt first. If you can't refinance your debt, pay off the highest interest rate loans first. These will cost you the most in the long run.

Use credit cards cautiously. They can be a convenient substitute for cash, but you need to be disciplined and pay them off every month to avoid more debt. If you can't pay them off immediately, pledge to pay them off completely in two or three months and recheck your spending habits.

Find ways to save. Once you are debt free, look into ways you can save your money instead of how you can spend it.

NEED HELP?

Sometimes you can't get out of debt. Situations beyond your control can arise and overwhelm you. Uninsured medical bills, unemployment, or a loss of business can happen to anyone. Many lenders will offer help and protection if you genuinely try to remedy the situation.

47 Saving your money will increase your buying power in the long run.

CONTACT LENDERS

To rebuild your credit record. If you stay on good terms with your creditors while you are delinquent, they are far more willing to help you rebuild credit. The creditor who reported it is the only one who can remove negative marks from your credit report. Get any agreements with creditors in writing. Send a copy of the written agreement to the bureau as backup.

Try the creditor again. If you've tried to correct errors or disputes in your credit report and the credit bureau isn't meeting your satisfaction, don't waste time. Contact the creditor directly and try to work it out with them. If you're successful, a letter to the credit bureau accompanied by the creditor's agreement in writing should resolve the problem.

DON'T BURY YOUR HEAD ▼
The simple act of facing your creditors and working out a plan can keep them from reporting the situation to a credit bureau—and keep your creditworthiness intact.

TALK WITH CREDITORS

Late notices. If you're late paying, creditors typically send you form letters as polite reminders. If you still don't pay, they may send more letters with increasing intensity or they may call you on the phone. Eventually the creditor will make demands, backed by the threat of action (a lawsuit or collection process).

They want you to work it out. Your creditors are motivated by two needs: to be repaid and to keep you as a customer. This tends to work in your favor. Legally, as soon as you default on a debt, the creditor has the right to ask you to repay the entire debt. That rarely happens, because the lender is interested in building a relationship with you and making more loans, not in ruining your credit record.

If you expect to pay late. Most creditors are willing to listen if you ask for help in structuring a new repayment plan. For example, they may grant you an extension of time or reduce payment amounts (but increase the number of payments).

Call to set up payment plans. Contact a lender as soon as you realize you won't be able to make a payment. Utilities, such as gas, electric, and phone, have payment plans already in place for people who have difficulty paying.

BANKRUPTCY

You can go to court for help in protecting your assets while you try to pay off your debts. This is the choice of last resort. First, you need to determine what type of bankruptcy plan is best for you. There are two choices.

WHAT IS BANKRUPTCY?

Bankruptcy is a legal declaration of your inability to repay your debts. When you file for bankruptcy you are telling your creditors you cannot pay them back at this time, but you are putting together a plan to pay them back partially or fully. Your creditors will be more interested in finding a way to get back their money than in forcing you into bankruptcy. Although you would prefer to avoid the intrusion, stigma, and future credit problems bankruptcy brings, sometimes it's the best solution. Once you apply to the courts, all collection efforts against you must stop. You're not allowed to take on any new debts, and the court freezes your assets.

48 Bankruptcy protects you from creditors while you reorganize your debts.

THE COURT CREATES YOUR PLAN

You can apply for Chapter 7 bankruptcy by asking the court to create a workable plan and carry it out for you. Your assets are frozen and a court appointed person (a *trustee*) takes control of your finances. The trustee's job is to review your assets, income, and debts, and then create the plan to distribute your assets to creditors as fairly as possible and in an orderly manner.

Depending on your state's law, you will be allowed to keep a certain amount of *exempt* property in order to maintain a reasonable, modest lifestyle. Your income will be protected so you can continue to support your family.

Once your assets have been distributed, the balance of your debts will be forgiven, except for certain obligations such as child support, alimony, and criminal liability. It would be bad public policy to allow you to avoid them.

At the end, depending on your circumstances, you could be debt free. But you will also have a damaged credit record that will take some time and good faith to rebuild.

SPECIAL PAYMENT PLANS

If you have a specific debt you would prefer to repay on your own instead of having the court get involved, you need to work out a *reaffirmation* plan with the court. This plan allows you to keep the item involved in the loan, such as your car, and repay the loan under new terms.

YOU CREATE YOUR PLAN

Applying for Chapter 13 protection in order to create your own plan gives you more flexibility than Chapter 7 to resolve your debts as you see fit.

After filing, you present the court with your own plan to repay your creditors, usually within 3-5 years. You must pledge all your disposable income (what's left after reasonable living expenses) to the plan.

If the court accepts your plan, you will make your payments to the court appointed trustee who will monitor your situation and distribute the money to your creditors. At the end of the process, you will be allowed to keep your remaining property, and the balance of any debts will be wiped out (unless forbidden by law). If the court doesn't accept your plan, you can resubmit another plan or switch to Chapter 7.

MORE ABOUT BANKRUPTCY

*H*ere is how to file for bankruptcy and what it means to your credit history. Be sure you understand all the advantages and disadvantages before you file.

HOW TO FILE

Get the forms and fill them out. Good professional guidance is advisable. If you really can't afford a lawyer or other professional, you can try using forms from the local court. They may be able to suggest low cost or free assistance to help you with your filing. It's worth asking. You will be asked to verify your:

- Income and property owned;
- Debts;
- Monthly living expenses;
- Property you're claiming as exempt.

File the forms with the local court. Although amounts may vary from state to state, expect the filing fee to be approximately $200.

Attend a creditors' meeting. After you've filed and the court has reviewed your case, you will be required to attend a creditors' meeting and face the people you owe. The creditors can show up and state their cases before the trustee, who then decides what's to be done. Since there usually isn't enough money for everyone, creditors usually must accept a fraction of what they're owed. This is the worst result of breaking your promise to repay because it breaks the bond of trust going forward.

FRAUD ALERT

Bankruptcy courts know that some people try to use them to avoid debts and keep their money. If you've transferred property, withdrawn lots of cash, or bought luxury items just before you file for bankruptcy, a court will investigate the possibility that you committed fraud. If the creditor finds out, it will probably pursue whatever remedies it has.

49 Creditors with secured loans are first in line to be repaid from the sale of property.

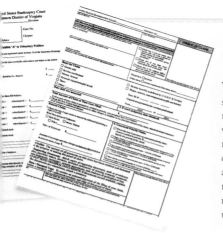

REESTABLISHING YOUR CREDIT

When you begin applying for credit again, some lenders will consider you too great a risk. Any lender who does offer you credit will insist on charging you a higher interest rate for the loan than they would offer more creditworthy borrowers. By using tools such as secured credit cards, you can gradually rebuild a positive credit profile. But you may not be considered a good credit risk until that ten-year period expires.

WHAT YOU MAY KEEP

Some debts are dischargeable (they can be forgiven) and some are not. Some assets are exempt (they can't be used to repay debts), and others are not. Here's a partial list.

Debts

- Dischargeable. Back rent, utility bills, personal loans, legal bills, accounting fines, and court judgments;
- Not dischargeable. Alimony, credit card charges, child support, tax obligations, student loans, or medical bills.

Assets

- Exempt. Your main car, tools of your trade, food, clothes, and family heirlooms;
- Not exempt. Luxury items, personal property, investments, or cash.

50 You may file for Chapter 7 only once every six years. There's no limit on filing for Chapter 13.

BANKRUPTCY ON YOUR CREDIT REPORT

A notice that you filed for Chapter 13 (a plan you create) stays on your credit report for seven years. A notice that you filed for Chapter 7 (the court-created plan) stays on your credit report for 10 years. Most consumer debt drops off of a credit report after seven years.

INDEX

ACKNOWLEDGMENTS

AUTHORS' ACKNOWLEDGMENTS

The production of this book has called on the skills of many people. We would like particularly to mention our editors at Dorling Kindersley, and our consultant, Nick Clemente. Marc wishes to dedicate this book to Zachary Robinson for his great patience and support when it was most needed.

PUBLISHER'S ACKNOWLEDGMENTS

Dorling Kindersley would like to thank everyone who generously lent props for the photoshoots, and the following for their help and participation:

Editorial Stephanie Rubenstein; **Design and Layout** Hedayat Sandjari; **Consultants** Nick Clemente; Skeeter; **Indexer** Rachel Rice; **Proofreader** Ruth Strother; **Photography** Anthony Nex; **Photographers' assistants** Victor Boghassian; Stephanie Fowler; **Models** Zachary Robinson; Kara Rubenstein; Victor Boghassian; Stephanie Rubenstein; **Preflighting** Mark Schroeder; **Picture researchers** Mark Dennis, Sam Ruston;

Special thanks to Teresa Clavasquin for her generous support and assistance.

AUTHORS' BIOGRAPHIES

Robert McKinley is the founder and chief executive of Maryland-based CardWeb.com Inc. and London-based RAM Research Group. Both firms track the payment card industry, provide competitive information to the card industry, and provide comparative information to consumers. Mr. McKinley is a nationally recognized authority on consumer credit and has provided expert testimony in major industry litigation cases and congressional hearings. He is highly regarded by the national news media as a reliable source of credible data with the ability to speak fairly to consumer issues as well as business issues pertaining to the credit industry.

Marc Robinson is co-founder of Internet-based moneytours.com, a personal finance resource for corporations, universities, credit unions, and other institutions interested in helping their constituents make intelligent decisions about their financial lives. He wrote the original *The Wall Street Journal Guide to Understanding Money and Markets*, created *The Wall Street Journal Guide to Understanding Personal Finance*, co-published a personal finance series with Time Life Books, and wrote a children's book about onomatopoeia in different languages. In his two decades in the financial services industry, Marc has provided marketing consulting to many top Wall Street firms. He is admitted to practice law in New York State.